Math Made Easy

10 Minutes A Day Math

Grade 1

Math Workbook

Author Deborah Lock
Consultant Alison Tribley

This timer counts up to 10 minutes.
When it reaches 10:00 it will beep.

How to use the timer:
Switch the timer ON.
Press the triangle ▶ to START the timer.
Press the square ■ to STOP or PAUSE the timer.
Press the square ■ to RESET the timer to 00:00.
Press any button to WAKE UP the timer.

LONDON, NEW YORK, MUNICH,
MELBOURNE, and DELHI

US Editor Nancy Ellwood
US Math Consultant Alison Tribley

Managing Art Editor Richard Czapnik
Art Director Martin Wilson
Pre-production Francesca Wardell

DK Delhi
Asst. Editor Nishtha Kapil
Asst. Art Editor Tanvi Nathyal
DTP Designer Anita Yadav
Dy. Managing Editor Soma B. Chowdhury
Design Consultant Shefali Upadhyay

First American Edition, 2014
Published in the United States by DK Publishing
345 Hudson Street, New York, New York 10014

14 15 16 17 10 9 8 7 6 5 4 3 2 1
001—195924—01/14

A catalog record for this book
is available from the Library of Congress
ISBN: 978-1-4654-1716-9

DK books are available at special discounts when purchased in bulk
for sales promotions, premiums, fund-raising, or educational use.
For details, contact:
DK Publishing Special Markets
345 Hudson Street, New York, New York 10014
SpecialSales@dk.com

Printed and bound in China by Leo Paper Products Ltd.
Timer designed and made in Hong Kong by Tritech

All images © Dorling Kindersley Limited
For further information see: www.dkimages.com
Discover more at
www.dk.com

Contents

Time Taken

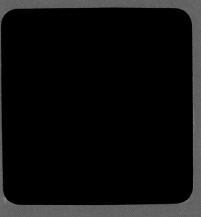

Time Filler:
In these boxes are some extra challenges to extend your skills. You can do them if you have some time left after finishing the questions. Or these can be stand-alone activities that you can do in 10 minutes.

Place Value

18 is 1 ten and 8 ones.
Now it is your turn.

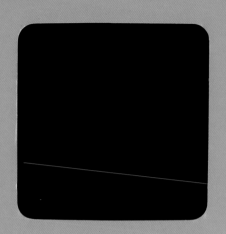

① Write 13 in words.

thirten

② What number is this?

28

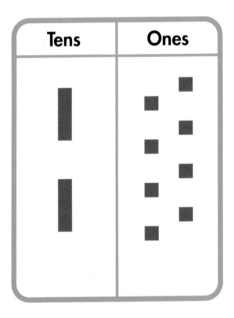

Tens	Ones

③ Write these numbers as digits.

fifteen 15

thirty-six 3 6

twenty  20

forty-five  4 5

4 Draw pictures for these numbers. Use these blocks.

Ten = | One = ■

7

Tens	Ones

17

Tens	Ones

27

Tens	Ones

5 How many tens are there in these numbers?

16 ....   34 ....   50 ....

27 ....   62 ....   85 ....

Length
Look around you. What is short and what is long?

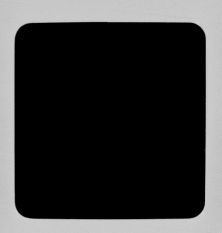

1 Which is longer? Check (✔) the answer.

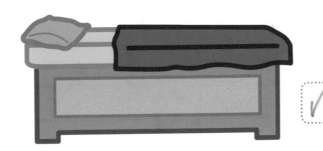 

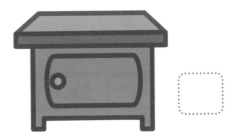

2 How many paperclips high is the book?

 paperclips

3 Which is shorter? Check (✔) the answer.

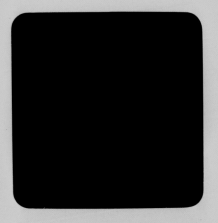

Time Filler:
Search around your home.
Can you find objects as long
as your finger, your hand,
and your arm?

(4) Draw these objects in order of size. Start with the shortest.

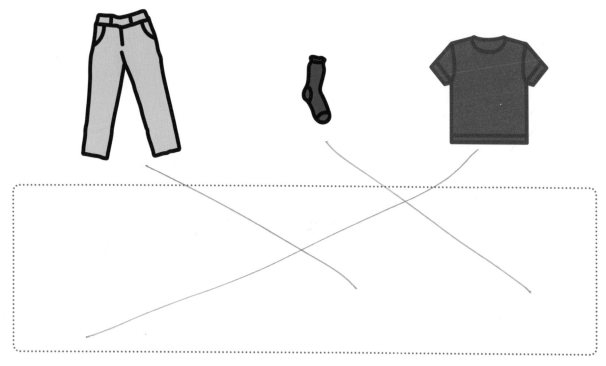

(5) Which is longer? Check (✔) the answer.

A shoe 5

A glove 4

Counting
Are you ready to count?
Press start.

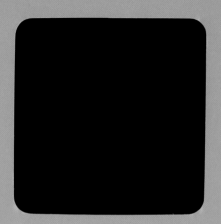

(1) Fill in the gaps.

5   6   *7*   8   *9*   *10*   *11*   12   13   *14*   15

(2) Count the fruits.

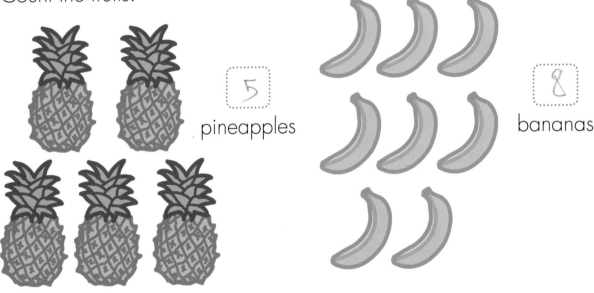

5 pineapples

8 bananas

16 cherries

(3) How many letters are there in your first name?

_____7_____

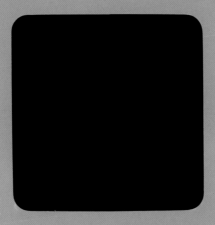

Time Filler:
Count as you do 10 hops,
20 skips, and 30 jumps.
Can you count to 50?

④ Draw the correct number of fruits.

9 pears

12 apples

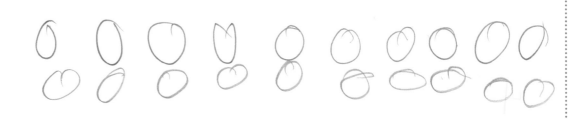

20 oranges

⑤ Fill in the gaps.

32   33   34   35   36   37   38   39   40   41   42

2-D Shapes

Many flat shapes have
sides and corners.

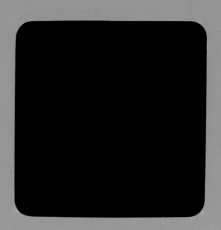

① Circle the triangles.

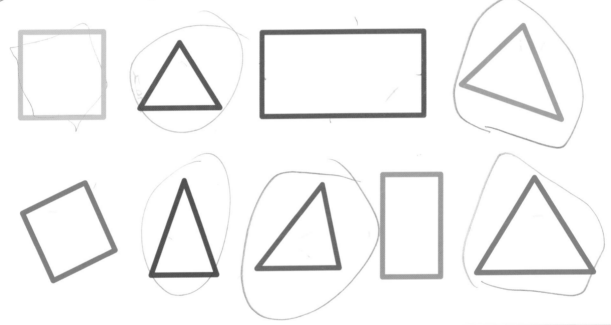

② How many corners does a square have?

 corners

③ Use a ruler to draw a rectangle.

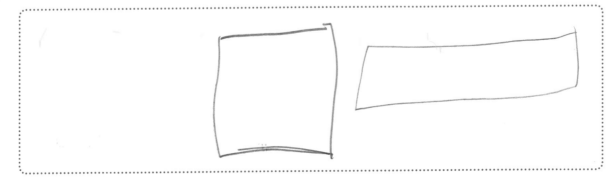

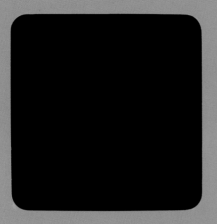

Time Filler:
What shape is the ON button
on the timer?
What shape is the STOP button?

4 Circle the shapes with four sides.

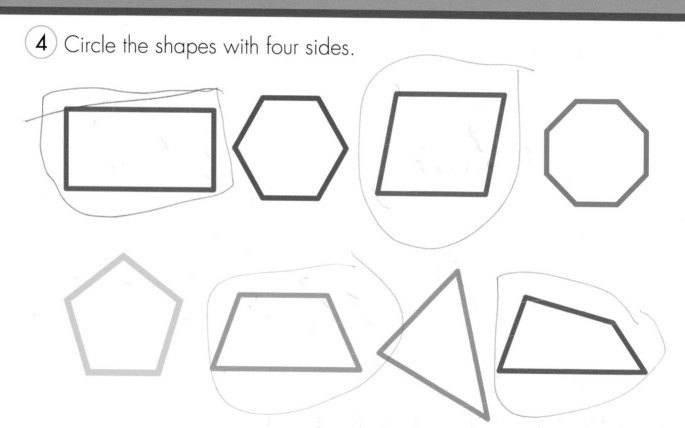

5 How many corners do these shapes have?

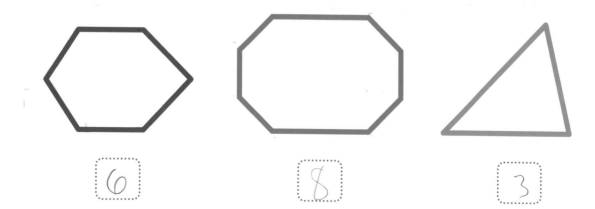

6   8   3

Counting in Leaps

Here is some more counting fun.
This time you leap over numbers!

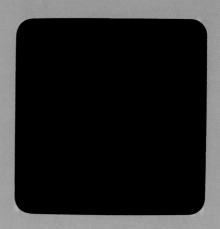

1 Count in 2s. Fill in the gaps.

1   3   5   7   9   11   13   15   17   19

2 Here is a number line. Start at 0 and show the leaps
you make when you count in 3s.

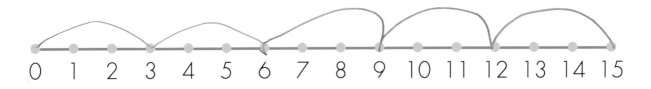

0 1 2 3 4 5 6 7 8 9 10 11 12 13 14 15

3 Count in 10s. Fill in the gaps.

10   20   30   40   50   60   70   80

6   16   26   36   46   56   66   76

25   35   45   55   65   75   85   95

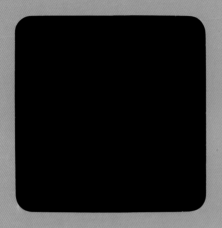

Time Filler:
Write all the numbers from 0 to 20
on a number line. Start from 0.
Which numbers do you land
on if you count in 5s?

④ What is 5 more than each of these numbers?

20 〔25〕   35 〔40〕   60 〔65〕

25 〔30〕   40 〔45〕   55 〔60〕

⑤ Count backward from 100 to 10. Count in 10s.

Tables and Graphs

See how quickly you can
find the information
on this table.

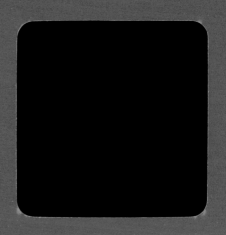

20 children were each asked to choose an ice cream flavor.
The results are shown on this table.

Flavor of Ice Cream	Number of Children
Vanilla	5
Chocolate	7
Strawberry	5
Raspberry	3

① Which was the most popular flavor?

Chocolate

② Which flavors had the same number?

Vanilla-strawberry

③ How many children chose vanilla?

5 children

Time Filler:
What ice cream flavors do you
and your friends like best?
Collect the data and make
your own bar graph.

(4) Look at the table opposite and color the correct number
of rectangles on the bar graph below.

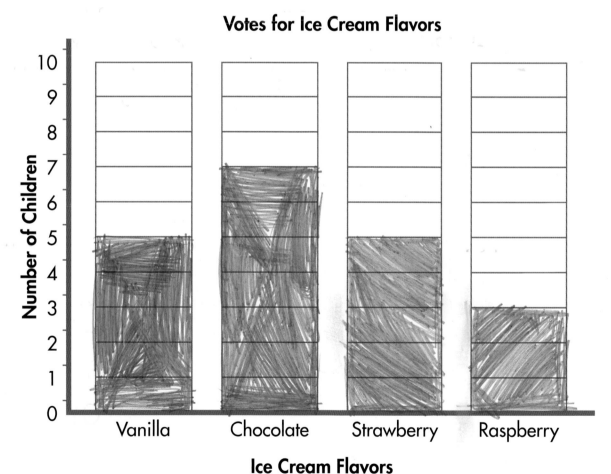

Votes for Ice Cream Flavors

Number of Children

10
9
8
7
6
5
4
3
2
1
0

Vanilla   Chocolate   Strawberry   Raspberry

Ice Cream Flavors

(5) Look at the graph above. How many more children chose
strawberry than raspberry ?

2   children

Number Fun

A 100 square or a number
line can help you answer
these questions.

---

(1) Put these numbers in the right order.
Start with the smallest.

67   85   24   7   36

| 7 | 24 | 36 | 67 | 85 |

---

(2) What is 1 more than these numbers?

11 **12**   25 **26**   73 **74**

88 **89**   99 **100**   49 **50**

---

(3) Circle the largest number in each pair.

4 or **(6)**   **(22)** or 17   8 or **(28)**

9 or **(19)**   **(35)** or 34   **(46)** or 29

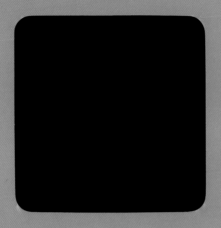

Time Filler:
What are the ages of your family members? Write the ages in order from the youngest to the oldest.

(4) What is 10 less than these numbers?

26   1 6   22   1 2   18   8

30   20   41   2 1   75   65

(5) Circle these numbers on the number lines below:

17   23   14   28   20

10 11 12 13 14 15 16 17 18 19 20 21 22 23 24 25 26 27 28 29 30

34   42   38   45   31

30 31 32 33 34 35 36 37 38 39 40 41 42 43 44 45 46 47 48 49 50

Combined 2-D Shapes

When shapes are combined,
they leave no gaps.

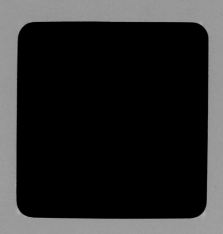

1 Draw a line to turn this shape into 2 rectangles.

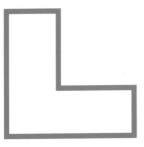

2 How many triangles can you make in this shape?

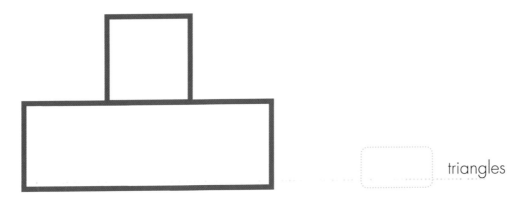

.... triangles

3 Can this shape be folded exactly in half? Circle Yes or No.

Yes   No

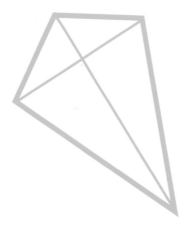

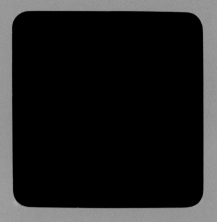

Time Filler:
How many different shapes can you make using 2 squares, 2 triangles, and 1 rectangle?

④ Draw your own shape using 2 triangles and 1 square.

⑤ Complete the picture by drawing the other half.
Note: The two halves look the same.

Beat the Clock 1

How many number words
do you know? Write them
as digits.

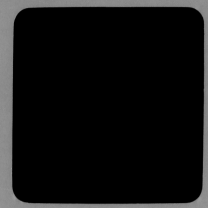

(1) Eleven

(2) Five

(3) Sixty

(4) Seventeen

(5) Forty-six

(6) Eighty

(7) Thirteen

(8) Eighty-seven

(9) Fifty

(10) Twenty-two

(11) Fifty-seven

(12) Sixty-four

(13) Seven

(14) Ninety-two

(15) Twelve

(16) Fifteen

(17) Ten

(18) Four

(19) Eighteen

(20) Forty-nine

(21) Sixty-one

(22) Forty-one

(23) Thirty-nine

(24) Ninety-three

(25) Seventy-seven

(26) Eighty-three

(27) Twenty-four

(28) One hundred

(29) Twenty-one

(30) Thirty-two

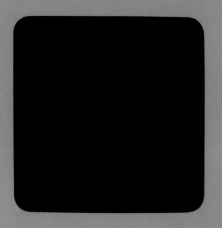

Time Filler:
The answers are on page 80.
Check if you were right.
Do this page another time
to try to beat your time.

(31) Three

(32) Nine

(33) Sixty-six

(34) Twenty-nine

(35) Two

(36) Twenty

(37) Thirty-eight

(38) Six

(39) Fifty-five

(40) Forty-four

(41) Seventy-eight

(42) Eighty-one

(43) Thirty

(44) Nineteen

(45) Twenty-seven

(46) Fifty-two

(47) Ninety-eight

(48) Eight

(49) One

(50) Ninety-one

(51) Forty

(52) Thirty-five

(53) Sixteen

(54) Seventy-five

(55) Eighty-four

(56) Seventy-four

(57) Thirty-three

(58) Fifty-three

(59) Fourteen

(60) Fifty-nine

Adding

Remember: + is the adding sign.
Are you ready to give these
problems a try?

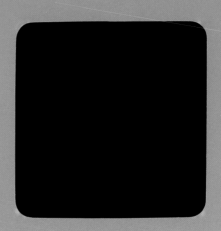

① Add up the items.

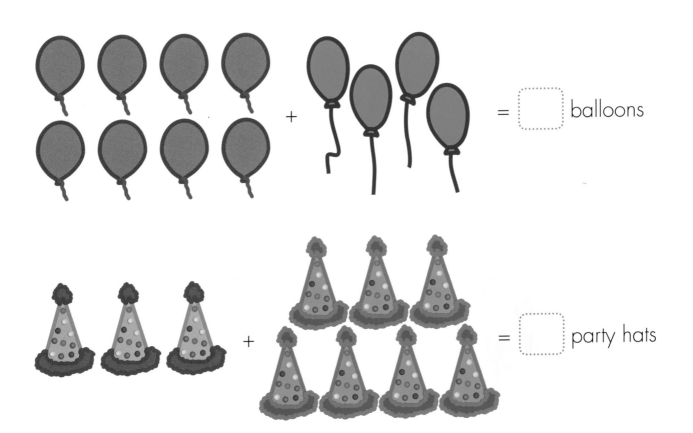

+ = [ ] balloons

+ = [ ] party hats

 +  = [ ] cupcakes

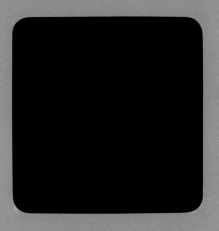

Time Filler:
How many T-shirts and pants
do you have altogether?

(2) Add these numbers.

10 + 6 = ☐   12 + 4 = ☐   15 + 3 = ☐

(3) Draw more candies to make 10 in each jar.

(4) What is the missing number?

3 + 4 + ☐ = 20

(5) Complete this number sentence.

If 8 + 3 = 11, then 3 + ☐ = 11

24

Weight

Look around you.
What is heavy?
What is light?

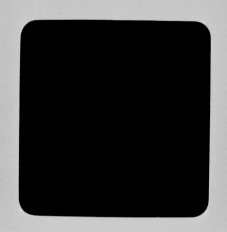

① Which is heavier? Check (✔) the answer.

 ☐    ☐

② How many rocks equal the weight of the cat?

☐ rocks

③ Which is lighter? Check (✔) the answer.

 ☐    ☐

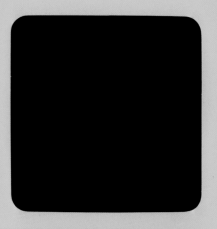

Time Filler:
Find three objects. Pick them up and feel their weight.
Which is the heaviest?
Which is the lightest?

④ Draw these animals in order of weight. Start with the lightest.

⑤ Which animal is heavier? Check (✔) the answer.

Subtracting

Someone has been eating
the cookies! There's fewer now.
Get started before they all go!

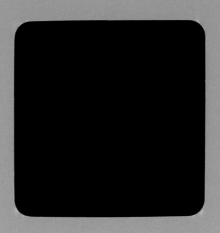

(1) How many cookies are left? The cookies that have
been eaten are crossed out.

 = [   ] cookies

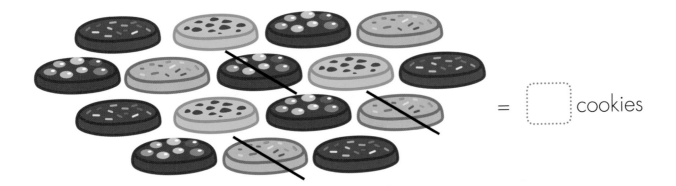 = [   ] cookies

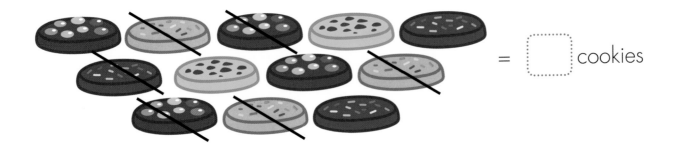 = [   ] cookies

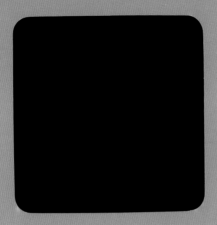

Time Filler:
Start with 20. Take away 5.
Subtract 3. What number is left?
Write your own problems and
try them out on a friend.

(2) Find the difference.

$7 - 6 =$ ⬚ $12 - 10 =$ ⬚ $15 - 7 =$ ⬚

(3) Use this number line to answer the questions.

0 1 2 3 4 5 6 7 8 9 10 11 12 13 14 15 16 17 18 19 20 21 22 23 24 25

What is 5 less than each number?

8 ⬚   10 ⬚   14 ⬚   20 ⬚   24 ⬚

(4) What is the missing number?

$20 - 4 -$ ⬚ $= 10$

(5) Complete this number sentence.

If $14 - 6 = 8$, then $14 -$ ⬚ $= 6$

3-D Shapes

Most 3-D shapes have faces, edges, and vertices (corners).

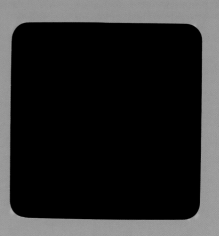

1 Circle the cones.

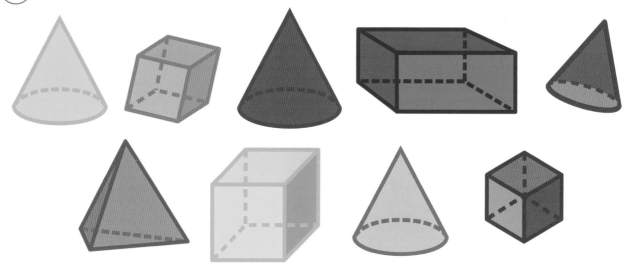

2 How many faces does a cube have? faces

3 How many edges do these shapes have?

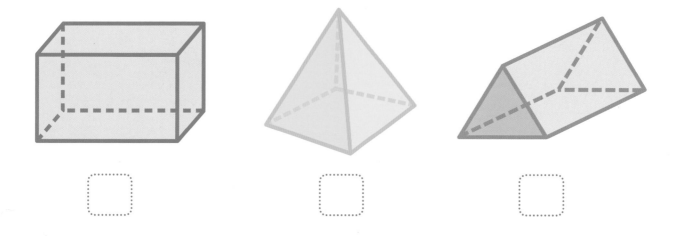

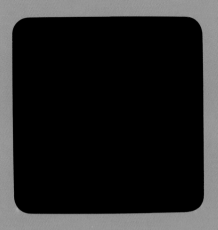

Time Filler:
Gather some empty boxes, paper towel rolls, and other packaging, and some glue or sticky tape. Make a model. Which 3-D shapes have you used?

4 Circle the shapes with eight vertices (corners).

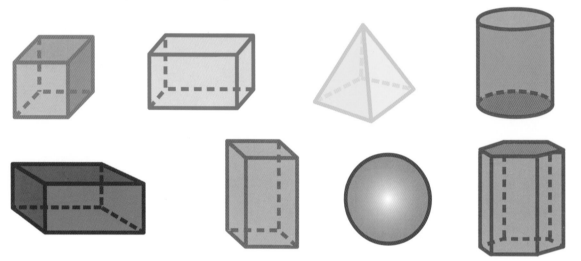

5 Draw a line from the name to the shape.

Cone

Sphere

Triangular Prism

Rectangular Prism

Hexagonal Prism

Sequences

Can you find the missing numbers?
Ready, set, go!

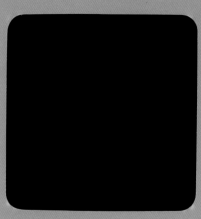

1 Double these numbers to complete the sequences.

| 2 | 4 | ⬚ | 16 | ⬚ | 64 |

| 3 | ⬚ | 12 | ⬚ | 48 | 96 |

2 Fill in the missing numbers.

| (+4) | 4 | ⬚ | ⬚ | ⬚ | 20 |

| (−3) | 27 | ⬚ | ⬚ | ⬚ | 15 |

| (+5) | 10 | ⬚ | ⬚ | ⬚ | 30 |

3 Write the next three even numbers.

| 12 | 14 | 16 | ⬚ | ⬚ | ⬚ |

| 34 | 36 | 38 | ⬚ | ⬚ | ⬚ |

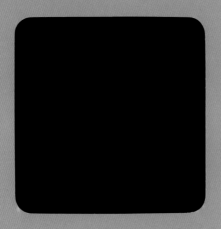

Time Filler:
Think of an odd number. Add 2.
Is your answer odd or even?
Think of an even number. Add 4.
Is your answer odd or even?

④ Circle the odd numbers in this sequence.

3   6   9   12   15

⑤ Look at the numbers on these doors.
Color the doors with odd numbers red
and those with even numbers green.

Telling Time

How much time will you take
to answer these time questions?
Start the timer!

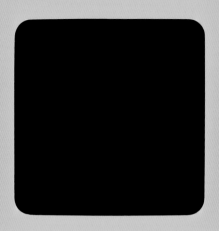

---

(1) What time is it?

---

(2) How many hours are there between these afternoon times?

---

(3) How many minutes are there in half an hour?

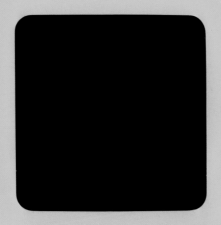

Time Filler:
Can you estimate 1 minute?
Close your eyes. Start the timer
and count to 60. Open your eyes
and stop the timer. Does the timer
read 01:00?

4 Show these times on the clocks.

4:30

5:00

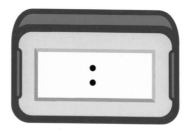

7:30

5 The school clock says 2:30 in the afternoon. School ends at
3 o'clock. How many minutes are there before school ends?

More Adding

Here is some more adding fun.
Get ready, and go!

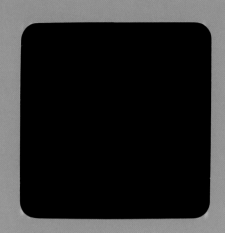

(1) How many cookies are there?

 +  = [ ] cookies

 + = [ ] cookies

 + = [ ] cookies

(2) Add these numbers.

14 + 5 = [ ]   11 + 9 = [ ]

15 + 2 = [ ]   13 + 7 = [ ]

(3) Fill in the missing numbers.

14 + [ ] = 20   8 + [ ] = 20

16 + [ ] = 20   17 + [ ] = 20

(4) This machine adds 10 to numbers. Add 10 to the numbers going IN and write the answers coming OUT.

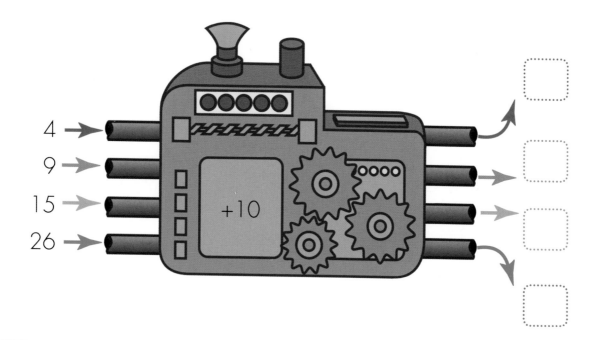

4 →
9 →
15 →
26 →

+10

(5) Here is a number line. Start at 3 and show the leaps you make when you count in 10s.

0 1 2 3 4 5 6 7 8 9 10 11 12 13 14 15 16 17 18 19 20 21 22 23 24 25

Patterns

Can you spot the patterns
and keep them going?
Let's find out.

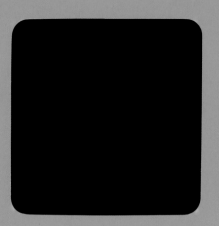

1 Continue the pattern.

....

2 Continue this pattern of numbers.

2   1   0   2   1   0   2   ☐   ☐   ☐

3 Look at the pattern of stones. Start from the house.

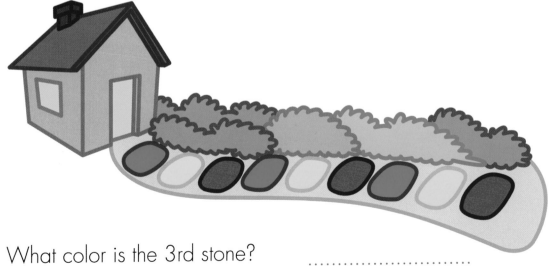

What color is the 3rd stone?   ....

What color is the 5th stone?   ....

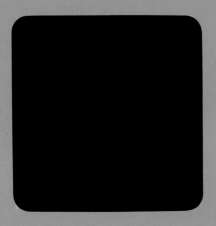

Time Filler:
Design a birthday card with your own pattern. Use a few shapes and colors and keep the pattern going.

④ Continue the pattern on the rug.

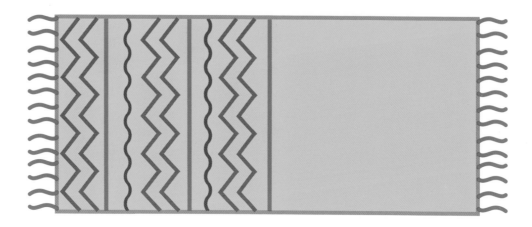

⑤ Fill in the gaps in this pattern.

More Subtracting

Here are some more subtraction problems to try out. Let's get started!

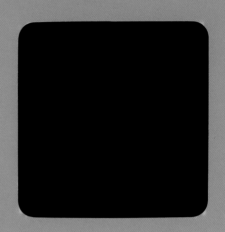

1 How many stars are left in each row?

— = ⬚ stars

— = ⬚ stars

— = ⬚ stars

2 Subtract.

14 – 5 = ⬚

11 – 9 = ⬚

15 – 10 = ⬚

13 – 6 = ⬚

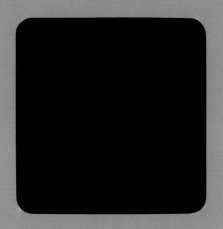

Time Filler:
Think of three numbers larger than 10.
What is 5 less than each of those numbers?

③ Fill in the missing numbers.

20 – ⬚ = 4   20 – ⬚ = 0

20 – ⬚ = 13   20 – ⬚ = 15

④ This machine takes away 10 from numbers.
Subtract 10 from the numbers going IN and write the
answers coming OUT.

14 →
19 →
25 →
36 →

⑤ Here is a number line. Start at 24 and show
the leaps to take away 4 each time.

0 1 2 3 4 5 6 7 8 9 10 11 12 13 14 15 16 17 18 19 20 21 22 23 24 25

Beat the Clock 2

Test your adding skills.
How many problems can
you do in 10 minutes?

(1) $2 + 3 =$ [ ]

(2) $7 + 4 =$ [ ]

(3) $3 + 3 + 3 =$ [ ]

(4) $6 + 2 =$ [ ]

(5) $6 + 6 =$ [ ]

(6) $6 + 3 + 8 =$ [ ]

(7) $7 + 1 =$ [ ]

(8) $7 + 3 =$ [ ]

(9) $2 + 5 + 6 =$ [ ]

(10) $8 + 5 =$ [ ]

(11) $6 + 4 =$ [ ]

(12) $4 + 4 + 4 =$ [ ]

(13) $3 + 8 =$ [ ]

(14) $8 + 8 =$ [ ]

(15) $7 + 7 + 6 =$ [ ]

(16) $6 + 8 =$ [ ]

(17) $4 + 3 =$ [ ]

(18) $2 + 7 + 5 =$ [ ]

(19) $3 + 3 =$ [ ]

(20) $6 + 7 =$ [ ]

(21) $5 + 5 + 5 =$ [ ]

(22) $5 + 3 =$ [ ]

(23) $8 + 5 =$ [ ]

(24) $8 + 8 + 2 =$ [ ]

(25) $6 + 5 =$ [ ]

(26) $7 + 8 =$ [ ]

(27) $3 + 7 + 3 =$ [ ]

(28) $6 + 9 =$ [ ]

(29) $9 + 9 =$ [ ]

(30) $6 + 6 + 10 =$ [ ]

Time Filler:
The answers are on page 80.
Check if you were right. Do this
page another time to try to beat
your time.

(31) 11 + 4 = ☐ (32) 12 + 7 = ☐ (33) 7 + 5 = ☐

(34) 16 + 2 = ☐ (35) 16 + 1 = ☐ (36) 7 + 9 = ☐

(37) 18 + 2 = ☐ (38) 11 + 7 = ☐ (39) 9 + 3 = ☐

(40) 12 + 8 = ☐ (41) 16 + 4 = ☐ (42) 6 + 3 = ☐

(43) 19 + 1 = ☐ (44) 18 + 4 = ☐ (45) 8 + 4 = ☐

(46) 11 + 1 = ☐ (47) 19 + 4 = ☐ (48) 12 + 3 = ☐

(49) 15 + 5 = ☐ (50) 14 + 6 = ☐ (51) 11 + 9 = ☐

(52) 17 + 1 = ☐ (53) 13 + 7 = ☐ (54) 14 + 5 = ☐

(55) 15 + 2 = ☐ (56) 13 + 5 = ☐ (57) 10 + 10 = ☐

(58) 11 + 3 = ☐ (59) 15 + 4 = ☐ (60) 18 + 10 = ☐

Counting Groups

Counting in groups is
a quick way to add.

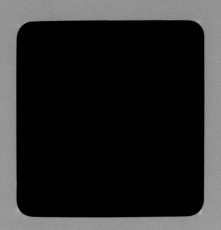

1. How many frogs are there?

☐ frogs

2. There are 4 grown-up rabbits. Each grown-up rabbit has
3 babies. How many rabbits are there in total?

☐ rabbits

3. How many birds are there?

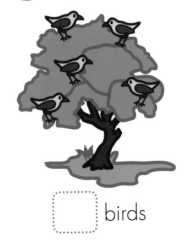  

☐ birds

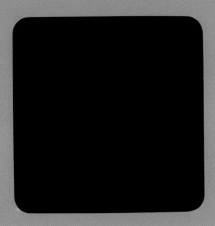

Time Filler:
Line up your shoes in pairs.
How many shoes do you
have altogether?

(4) Here are 20 monkeys. How many groups of 4 monkeys
can you make? Put a circle around each group.

[ ] groups

(5) How many toes are there on four feet?

 toes

Charts

Charts are a useful way
to find out data quickly.
Give it a try!

Kim made a chart of the weather in one week.

Days of the Week	Weather
Monday	☀
Tuesday	☁
Wednesday	☀
Thursday	🌧
Friday	☀
Saturday	☀
Sunday	☁

☀ = Sunny

🌧 = Rainy

☁ = Cloudy

(1) What was the weather like on Wednesday? ....

(2) How many days had rain? ....

(3) Which days were cloudy? ....

Time Filler:
What is the weather like today?
Design your own weather chart.
Record the weather for the week.

④ Use the chart opposite to fill in this bar graph.
Color in the number of days for each type of weather.

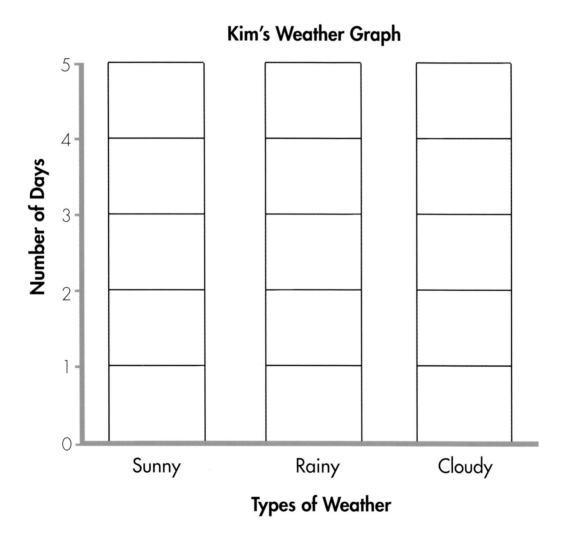

Kim's Weather Graph

⑤ How many more days had sun than rain?

. . . .

Money

Before you begin, keep
a pile of coins in front
of you to help you.

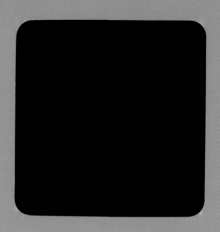

(1) Circle the two coins you would use to make 15¢.

(2) Decrease each amount by 5¢.
Note: To decrease we subtract.

10¢	20¢	25¢	50¢

(3) Increase each amount by 3¢.
Note: To increase we add.

10¢	20¢	25¢	40¢

Time Filler:
Choose three coins. Add them together to find their total. Choose three other coins and find their total. Which amount is larger?

(4) Which coins together equal the amount shown?
Write the amounts on the faces of the coins.

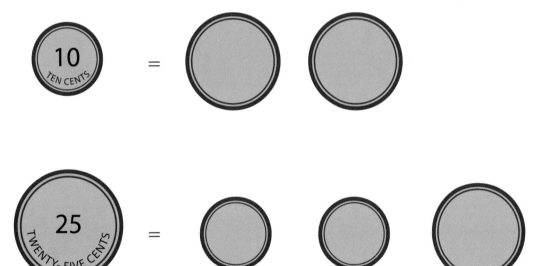

(5) Put these amounts in order, starting with the smallest.

25 ¢   13 ¢   42 ¢   8 ¢   20 ¢

Fractions of Shapes

Split these shapes into equal parts
to find the fractions.

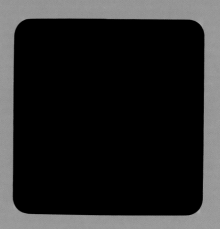

(1) Color half the circle.

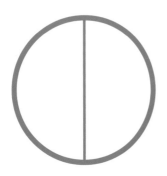

How many halves are
there in a whole circle?

(2) Color a quarter of the rectangle.

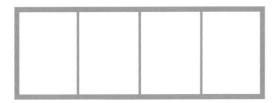

How many
quarters are there
in a rectangle?

(3) Check (✔) the fraction colored on this circle.

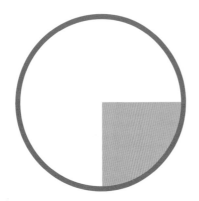

$\frac{1}{2}$ ☐ $\frac{1}{4}$ ☐

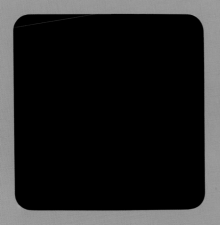

④ Look at these shapes. Check (✔) the shapes
that are half colored in.

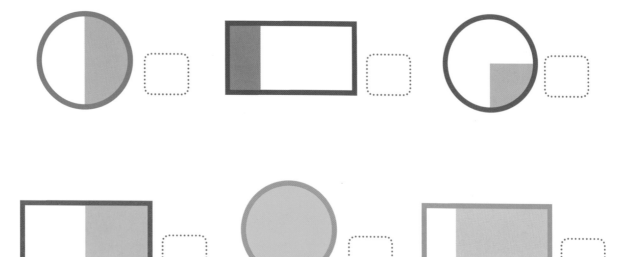

⑤ Write a half as a fraction. ⬚／⬚

Write a quarter as a fraction. ⬚／⬚

Solving Problems

Will you add or subtract?
Read each question carefully.

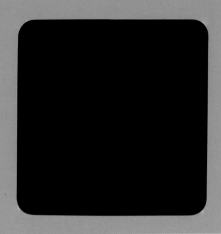

(1) James had 35 toy cars. John had 15 toy cars.
How many toy cars did they have together?

⬚ cars

(2) Mom bought 8 oranges.
Kate ate 2 of them. Jane ate 1.
How many oranges were left?

⬚ oranges

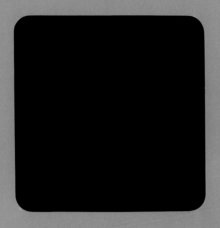

Time Filler:
Count the number of books you have.
Take away the ones with hard covers.
How many books are left?

3 A lady had 3 cats. Each cat had 2 kittens.
How many cats and kittens were there in total?

cats and kittens

4 Omar had 40 books. He gave
26 to the school and the rest
to charity. How many books
did he give to charity?

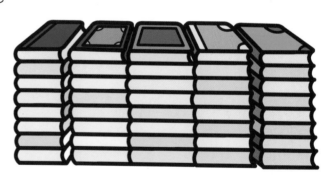

books

5 Dad cooked a pizza and cut it into
8 equal slices. He ate half of them.
How many slices were left?

slices

Shopping

It is useful to know how to add
and subtract money when shopping.
Give it a try!

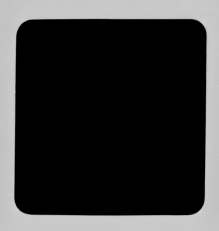

1 What is the total of these amounts?

1¢   +   5¢   +   10¢   +   25¢   =

$1   + $1   + $1   +   25¢   =

2 A lollipop costs 26¢. You pay with these coins:

How much change do you get?

3 Hedi and Henry have these coins:

Hedi

Henry

Whose coins are worth more money? ....

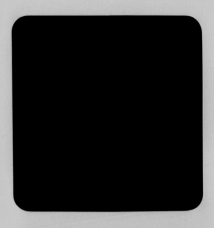

---

(4) How much change will you get from $1?

96 ¢

[ ]

---

(5) A woman buys 2 cartons of milk. How much change does she get from $2? Fill in the spaces to show your work.

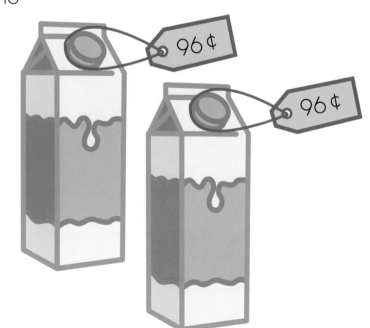

96 ¢

96 ¢

96 ¢ + 96 ¢ = [ ]

$2 − $1.92 = [ ]

Fractions of Amounts

Count the amounts. Then split
them into equal parts.

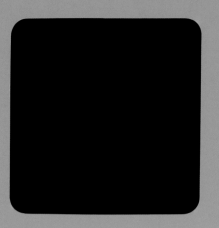

① Here are 6 balloons. Color in half of them.

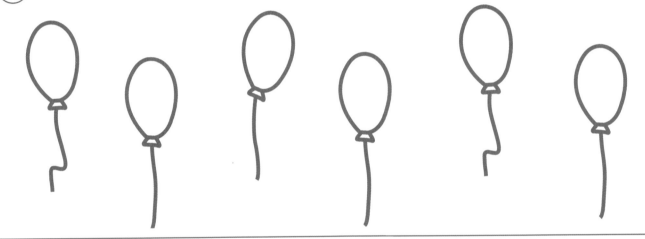

② How many minutes are there in a quarter of an hour?

③ What is a quarter of $1?

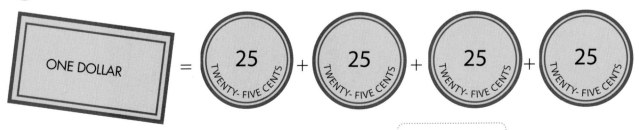

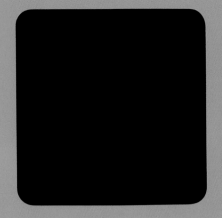

Time Filler:
Draw 10 circles. Color half of them in blue. How many circles are colored?

④ Here are 12 party hats. Color one quarter red, one quarter green, and half blue.

⑤ What is half of each number?

4   6   8   10

More Groups

How quickly can you count in groups? Start the timer when you are ready to go.

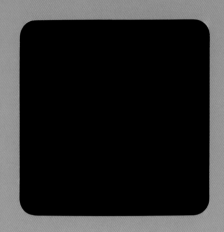

(1) How many fish are there?

 fish

(2) There are 3 turtles. Each turtle lays 5 eggs. How many eggs are there?

 eggs

(3) How many penguins are there?

penguins

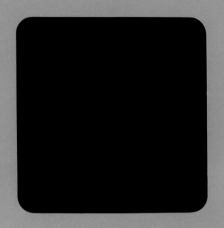

Time Filler:
Draw 4 groups of 3 fish. How many fish are there altogether?

(4) Here are 20 dolphins. How many groups of 5 dolphins can you make? Put a circle around each group.

 groups

(5) Write the answers.

2 groups of 7 =

3 groups of 10 =

4 groups of 5 =

5 groups of 3 =

58

More Time

Start the timer before you get going on this page. Time is ticking!

① What time is it?

② How many hours are there between these morning times?

③ Jade started reading at 5 o'clock. She read for an hour. What time did she finish reading?

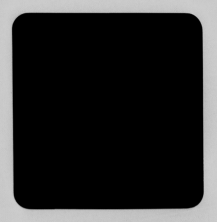

Time Filler:
Use the timer to find out how long it takes to do 10 jumps, 20 jumps, and 30 jumps.

④ Label this clock with numbers. Show 3 o'clock on the clock face.

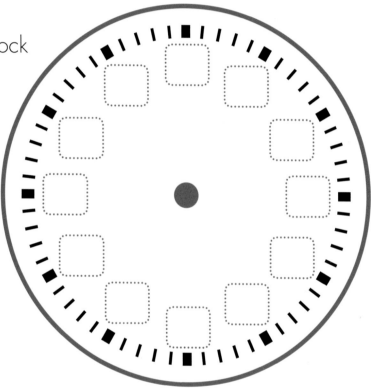

⑤ School starts at 8:30. Dan left home at 8:00. How many minutes does he have to get to school on time?

SCHOOL

Race Positions

Which car will be first past
the finishing line?

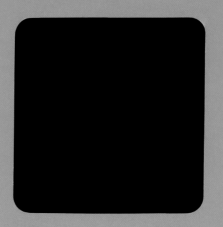

Six cars are racing.

(1) Which car is first?

....

(2) Which car is fourth?

....

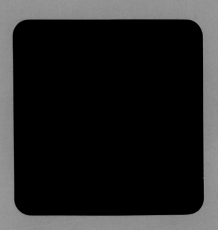

Time Filler:
Watch a car race on TV. How many cars raced? Who came in first?

 ③ In what place is the green car?

....

 ④ The cars line up in their finishing positions. Which car is fifth?

....

  ⑤ Which car is lined up in front of the blue car?

....

Position

Are you sitting on a chair?
What is beside you?

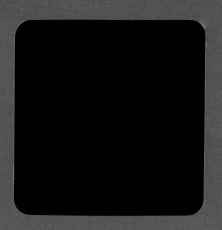

Look at this chart of animals.

① Which animal is above the mouse? ....

② Which animal is below the cat? ....

③ Which animal is beside the rabbit? ....

④ Which animal is between the duck and the dog? ....

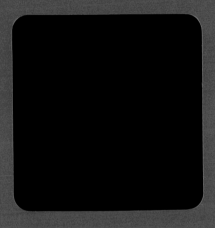

Time Filler:
Look inside a kitchen cabinet. Describe the position of the objects, using the words above, below, and beside.

(5) Draw the animals on this chart.

Draw a spider under the monkey.

Draw a butterfly below the frog.

Draw a snake next to the butterfly.

Draw a bird above the frog.

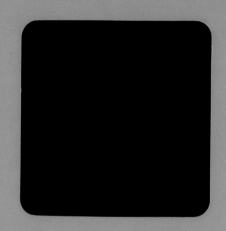

Beat the Clock 3

Test your subtracting skills.
How many problems can
you do in 10 minutes?

1 8 − 3 =

2 3 − 2 =

3 10 − 8 =

4 7 − 3 =

5 5 − 5 =

6 13 − 3 =

7 8 − 5 =

8 7 − 5 =

9 10 − 5 =

10 9 − 1 =

11 6 − 2 =

12 19 − 7 =

13 5 − 2 =

14 9 − 3 =

15 11 − 9 =

16 4 − 3 =

17 3 − 3 =

18 15 − 5 =

19 9 − 7 =

20 8 − 1 =

21 18 − 6 =

22 9 − 2 =

23 4 − 2 =

24 16 − 5 =

25 6 − 5 =

26 9 − 5 =

27 10 − 7 =

28 6 − 3 =

29 9 − 8 =

30 14 − 8 =

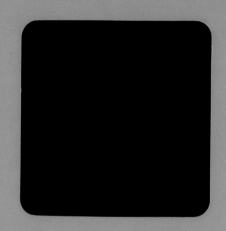

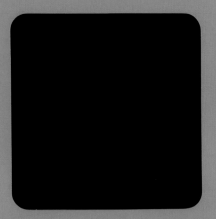

Time Filler:
The answers are on page 80. Check if you were right. Do this page another time to try to beat your time.

(31) 10 − 3 = ☐   (32) 17 − 6 = ☐   (33) 12 − 8 = ☐

(34) 15 − 4 = ☐   (35) 14 − 5 = ☐   (36) 18 − 9 = ☐

(37) 10 − 6 = ☐   (38) 16 − 3 = ☐   (39) 15 − 12 = ☐

(40) 14 − 7 = ☐   (41) 12 − 4 = ☐   (42) 16 − 12 = ☐

(43) 10 − 4 = ☐   (44) 10 − 1 = ☐   (45) 20 − 17 = ☐

(46) 13 − 6 = ☐   (47) 15 − 3 = ☐   (48) 20 − 12 = ☐

(49) 17 − 7 = ☐   (50) 14 − 3 = ☐   (51) 17 − 11 = ☐

(52) 12 − 6 = ☐   (53) 10 − 2 = ☐   (54) 15 − 13 = ☐

(55) 10 − 9 = ☐   (56) 15 − 8 = ☐   (57) 20 − 10 = ☐

(58) 9 − 4 = ☐   (59) 16 − 4 = ☐   (60) 20 − 15 = ☐

Answers:

4–5 Place Value
6–7 Length

4

① Write 13 in words.

_____ thirteen _____

② What number is this?

28

Tens	Ones

③ Write these numbers as digits.

fifteen — 15   thirty-six — 36

twenty — 20   forty-five — 45

5

④ Draw pictures for these numbers. Use these blocks.

Ten = ▮   One = ■

7

Tens	Ones

17

Tens	Ones

27

Tens	Ones

⑤ How many tens are there in these numbers?

16 — 1 ten   34 — 3 tens   50 — 5 tens

27 — 2 tens   62 — 6 tens   85 — 8 tens

By this time, children are beginning to think of whole numbers in terms of tens and ones. These activities help to build a sense of numbers and their size in relation to each other. Drawing tens as a long stick and ones as a small square is a useful visual aid.

6

① Which is longer? Check (✔) the answer.

✔

② How many paperclips high is the book?

4 paperclips

③ Which is shorter? Check (✔) the answer.

✔

7

④ Draw these objects in order of size. Start with the shortest.

⑤ Which is longer? Check (✔) the answer.

A shoe ✔   A glove

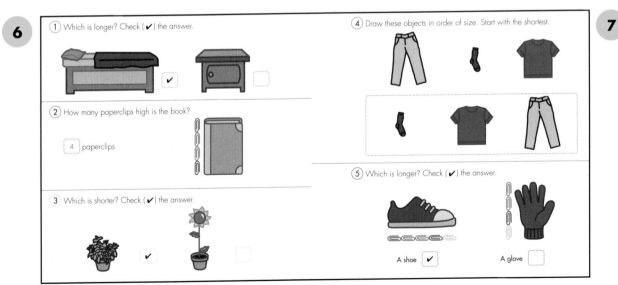

Children of this age are developing an understanding of the meaning and processes of measurement. These questions compare lengths of familiar objects, and help to measure the length of an object with familiar "units," such as paperclips.

Answers:

8–9 Counting
10–11 2-D Shapes

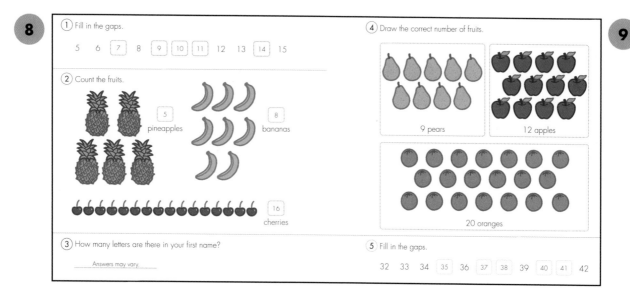

8

① Fill in the gaps.

5   6   [7]   8   [9]   [10]   [11]   12   13   [14]   15

② Count the fruits.

[5] pineapples
[8] bananas
[16] cherries

③ How many letters are there in your first name?

_____ Answers may vary.

9

④ Draw the correct number of fruits.

9 pears
12 apples
20 oranges

⑤ Fill in the gaps.

32   33   34   [35]   36   [37]   [38]   39   [40]   [41]   42

Children at this age need plenty of practice at counting objects and putting numbers in consecutive order. They should be confident of counting and writing numbers up to 20, and beginning to recognize numbers to 100.

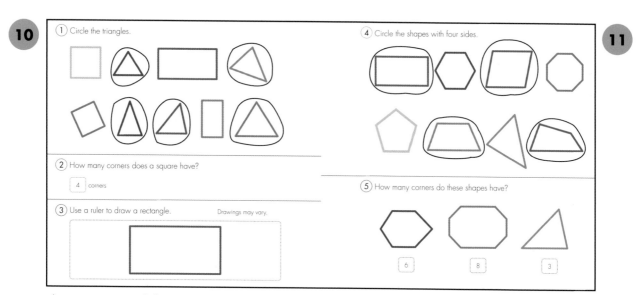

10

① Circle the triangles.

② How many corners does a square have?

[4] corners

③ Use a ruler to draw a rectangle.

Drawings may vary.

11

④ Circle the shapes with four sides.

⑤ How many corners do these shapes have?

[6]   [8]   [3]

Shapes are purposefully presented in different colors and orientation so that children can distinguish between their defining (sides, corners) and non-defining (color, size) features. Children also practice drawing shapes.

Answers:

12–13 Counting in Leaps
14–15 Tables and Graphs

12

① Count in 2s. Fill in the gaps.

1　3　[5]　7　9　[11]　[13]　15　[17]　19

② Here is a number line. Start at 0 and show the leaps you make when you count in 3s.

0　1　2　3　4　5　6　7　8　9　10　11　12　13　14　15

③ Count in 10s. Fill in the gaps.

10　20　[30]　[40]　50　60　[70]　80

6　16　[26]　36　[46]　[56]　66　[76]

25　[35]　45　55　[65]　75　[85]　95

13

④ What is 5 more than each of these numbers?

20　[25]　　35　[40]　　60　[65]

25　[30]　　40　[45]　　55　[60]

⑤ Count backward from 100 to 10. Count in 10s.

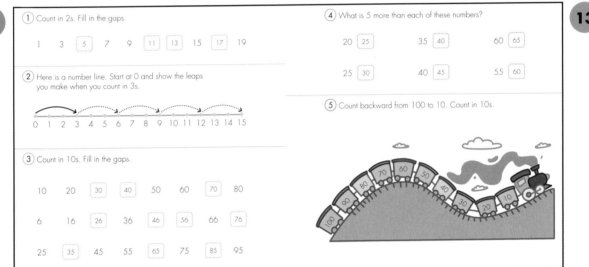

Counting in leaps is a step on the way to understanding addition. Counting in 10s forward and backward helps to reinforce the idea of the number of tens in place value. The numbers 10, 20, 30, and 40 refer to one, two, three, or four tens respectively.

14

20 children were each asked to choose an ice cream flavor. The results are shown on this table.

Flavor of Ice Cream	Number of Children
Vanilla	5
Chocolate	7
Strawberry	5
Raspberry	3

① Which was the most popular flavor?

chocolate

② Which flavors had the same number?

vanilla and strawberry

③ How many children chose vanilla?

[5] children

15

④ Look at the table opposite and color the correct number of rectangles on the bar graph below.

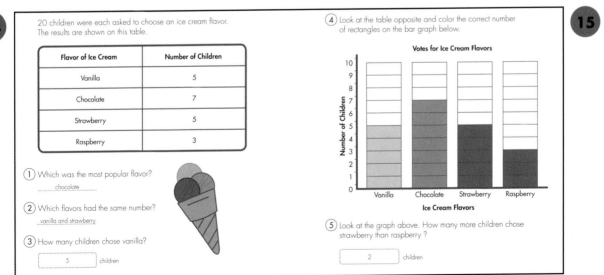

Votes for Ice Cream Flavors

⑤ Look at the graph above. How many more children chose strawberry than raspberry ?

[2] children

This activity aims to reinforce children's ability to read tables and to organize and represent data on bar graphs. Ice cream is a popular topic to choose.

Children need to compare the heights of the columns to find the last answer.

Answers:

16–17 Number Fun
18–19 Combined 2-D Shapes

16

① Put these numbers in the right order.
Start with the smallest.

67   85   24   7   36

| 7 | 24 | 36 | 67 | 85 |

② What is 1 more than these numbers?

11 [12]   25 [26]   73 [74]

88 [89]   99 [100]   49 [50]

③ Circle the largest number in each pair.

4 or ⑥   ㉒ or 17   8 or ㉘

9 or ⑲   ㉟ or 34   ㊻ or 29

17

④ What is 10 less than these numbers?

26 [16]   22 [12]   18 [8]

30 [20]   41 [31]   75 [65]

⑤ Circle these numbers on the number lines below:

17   23   14   28   20

10 11 12 13 ⑭ 15 16 ⑰ 18 19 ⑳ 21 22 ㉓ 24 25 26 27 ㉘ 29 30

34   42   38   45   31

30 ㉛ 32 33 ㉞ 35 36 37 ㊳ 39 40 41 ㊷ 43 44 ㊺ 46 47 48 49 50

These pages practice a range of number skills: ordering numbers, comparing the size of numbers, finding them on a number line, and adding and subtracting one and ten. Write your own similar questions and get your child to practicing his/her number skills.

18

① Draw a line to turn this shape into 2 rectangles.

or

② How many triangles can you make in this shape?   Answers may vary.

[16] triangles

③ Can this shape be folded exactly in half? Circle Yes or No.

(Yes)   No

19

④ Draw your own shape using 2 triangles and 1 square.
Drawings may vary.

⑤ Complete the picture by drawing the other half.
Note: The two halves look the same.

Working with shapes at this stage is fun for kids. Children are asked to combine two-dimensional shapes to make composite shapes. It is helpful to have an assortment of shapes handy, perhaps cut out from a cardboard cereal box, so your child can practice composing new shapes.

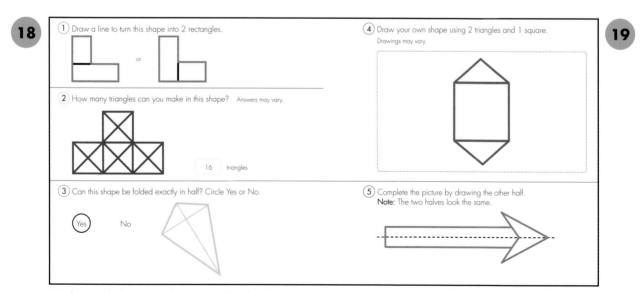

Answers:

22–23 Adding
24–25 Weight

22

① Add up the items.

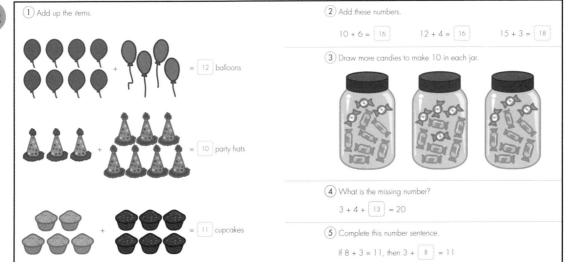

+ = 12 balloons

+ = 10 party hats

+ = 11 cupcakes

23

② Add these numbers.

10 + 6 = 16   12 + 4 = 16   15 + 3 = 18

③ Draw more candies to make 10 in each jar.

④ What is the missing number?

3 + 4 + 13 = 20

⑤ Complete this number sentence.

If 8 + 3 = 11, then 3 + 8 = 11

A variety of addition problems are practiced on these pages: counting objects and adding them together to find the total, adding within 20, and working with addition equations. Children should be applying strategies to add, such as knowing what numbers added together make 10.

24

① Which is heavier? Check (✔) the answer.

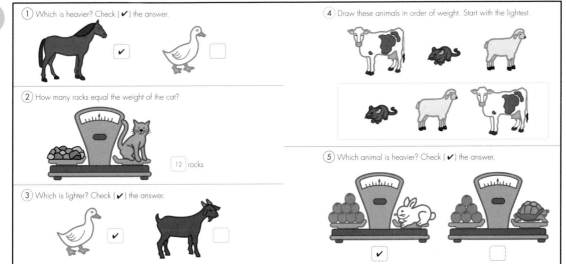

② How many rocks equal the weight of the cat?

12 rocks

③ Which is lighter? Check (✔) the answer.

25

④ Draw these animals in order of weight. Start with the lightest.

⑤ Which animal is heavier? Check (✔) the answer.

Children do not get much opportunity to learn about weights at this age. However, comparing the weights of different animals is a fun way to introduce the topic to them. Measuring the animal weights with a third object (oranges) is another type of comparison.

71

Answers:

26–27 Subtracting
28–29 3-D Shapes

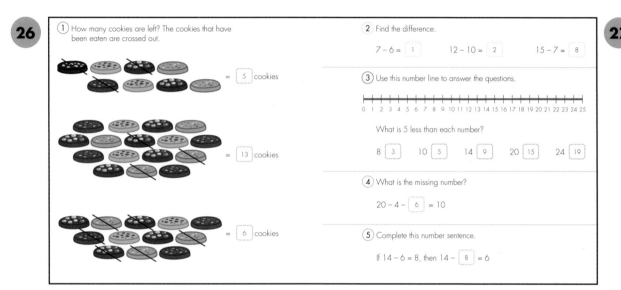

26

① How many cookies are left? The cookies that have been eaten are crossed out.

= 5 cookies

= 13 cookies

= 6 cookies

27

② Find the difference.

7 – 6 = 1   12 – 10 = 2   15 – 7 = 8

③ Use this number line to answer the questions.

0 1 2 3 4 5 6 7 8 9 10 11 12 13 14 15 16 17 18 19 20 21 22 23 24 25

What is 5 less than each number?

8 3   10 5   14 9   20 15   24 19

④ What is the missing number?

20 – 4 – 6 = 10

⑤ Complete this number sentence.

If 14 – 6 = 8, then 14 – 8 = 6

These pages will show how fluent your child is with subtraction. Crossing out objects and moving to the left on a number line provide visual support for the concept of taking away. Knowing the relationship between addition and subtraction is very useful: Ex. 3 + 7 = 10 is the same as 10 – 7 = 3.

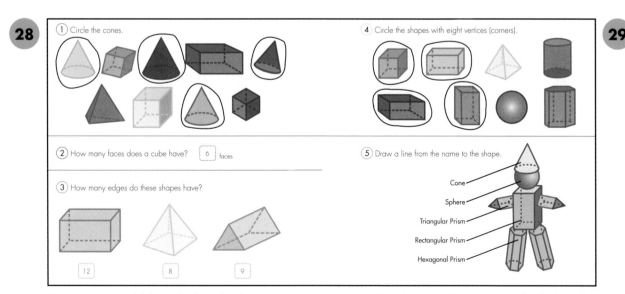

28

① Circle the cones.

② How many faces does a cube have? 6 faces

③ How many edges do these shapes have?

12   8   9

29

④ Circle the shapes with eight vertices (corners).

⑤ Draw a line from the name to the shape.

Cone
Sphere
Triangular Prism
Rectangular Prism
Hexagonal Prism

Encourage your child to talk about the three-dimensional shapes on these pages, comparing their attributes. If necessary, help your children count the edges and the vertices, and talk about flat bases and curved sides.

Answers:

30–31 Sequences
32–33 Telling Time

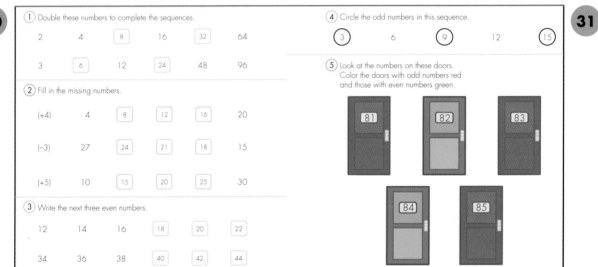

30

1 Double these numbers to complete the sequences.

| 2 | 4 | 8 | 16 | 32 | 64 |

| 3 | 6 | 12 | 24 | 48 | 96 |

2 Fill in the missing numbers.

(+4)	4	8	12	16	20
(–3)	27	24	21	18	15
(+5)	10	15	20	25	30

3 Write the next three even numbers.

| 12 | 14 | 16 | 18 | 20 | 22 |

| 34 | 36 | 38 | 40 | 42 | 44 |

31

4 Circle the odd numbers in this sequence.

3   6   9   12   15

5 Look at the numbers on these doors. Color the doors with odd numbers red and those with even numbers green.

81   82   83

84   85

Provide children with a number chart from 1–100 if they need visual support to complete these questions. Make sure children know that an even number ends in 0, 2, 4, 6, or 8 ones; and an odd number ends in 1, 3, 5, 7, or 9 ones.

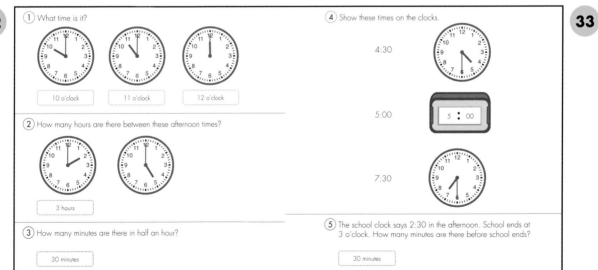

32

1 What time is it?

10 o'clock   11 o'clock   12 o'clock

2 How many hours are there between these afternoon times?

3 hours

3 How many minutes are there in half an hour?

30 minutes

33

4 Show these times on the clocks.

4:30

5:00   5 : 00

7:30

5 The school clock says 2:30 in the afternoon. School ends at 3 o'clock. How many minutes are there before school ends?

30 minutes

Children are taught to tell and write time in hours and half-hours using both analog and digital clocks. Look out for opportunities to talk about time with children, such as what time they leave the house for school and what time they go to bed.

Answers:

34–35 More Adding
36–37 Patterns

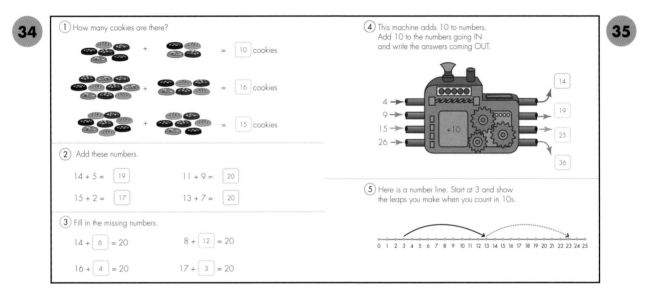

34

1. How many cookies are there?

🍪 + 🍪 = `10` cookies

🍪 + 🍪 = `16` cookies

🍪 + 🍪 = `15` cookies

2. Add these numbers.

14 + 5 = `19`   11 + 9 = `20`

15 + 2 = `17`   13 + 7 = `20`

3. Fill in the missing numbers.

14 + `6` = 20   8 + `12` = 20

16 + `4` = 20   17 + `3` = 20

35

4. This machine adds 10 to numbers. Add 10 to the numbers going IN and write the answers coming OUT.

4 →   → `14`
9 →   → `19`
15 → +10 → `25`
26 →   → `36`

5. Here is a number line. Start at 3 and show the leaps you make when you count in 10s.

0 1 2 3 4 5 6 7 8 9 10 11 12 13 14 15 16 17 18 19 20 21 22 23 24 25

The idea of the number machine encourages children to mentally find 10 more than the number going in. Explain that 10 has been added to the number. Keep practicing with children the different combinations of numbers to make 20

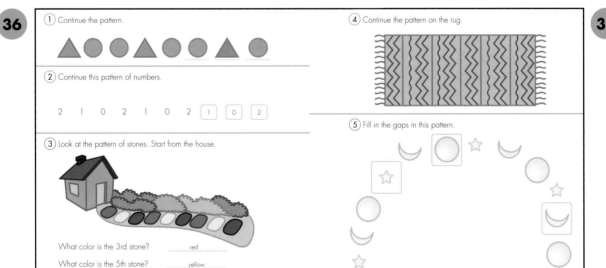

36

1. Continue the pattern.

△ ◯ ◯ △ ◯ △ ◯ ◯

2. Continue this pattern of numbers.

2 1 0 2 1 0 2 `1` `0` `2`

3. Look at the pattern of stones. Start from the house.

What color is the 3rd stone? .... red
What color is the 5th stone? .... yellow

37

4. Continue the pattern on the rug.

5. Fill in the gaps in this pattern.

Shape and color patterns help children think logically. Can your children spot the patterns and keep them going? Encourage children to draw their own shape and color patterns. Can they keep their patterns going?

Answers:

38–39 More Subtracting
42–43 Counting Groups

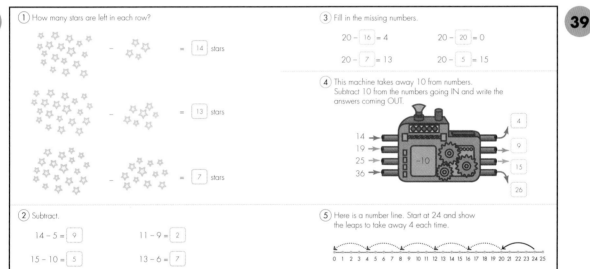

38

① How many stars are left in each row?

☆ ☆ ☆ ☆ ☆ — ☆ ☆ = [14] stars

☆ ☆ ☆ ☆ ☆ — ☆ ☆ = [13] stars

☆ ☆ ☆ ☆ ☆ — ☆ ☆ = [7] stars

② Subtract.

14 – 5 = [9]   11 – 9 = [2]

15 – 10 = [5]   13 – 6 = [7]

39

③ Fill in the missing numbers.

20 – [16] = 4   20 – [20] = 0

20 – [7] = 13   20 – [5] = 15

④ This machine takes away 10 from numbers. Subtract 10 from the numbers going IN and write the answers coming OUT.

14 →   → [4]
19 →   → [9]
25 →   –10   → [15]
36 →   → [26]

⑤ Here is a number line. Start at 24 and show the leaps to take away 4 each time.

0 1 2 3 4 5 6 7 8 9 10 11 12 13 14 15 16 17 18 19 20 21 22 23 24 25

If children need help with the first question, encourage them to cross out a star from each side of the subtraction sign. They should stop once the second group is all crossed out, and then count how many are left in the first group.

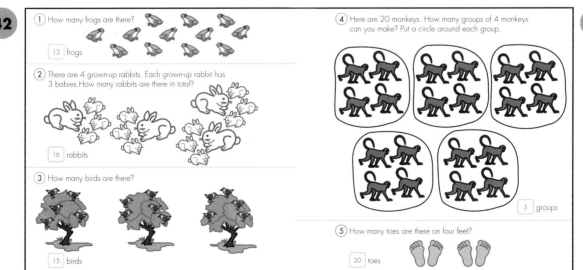

42

① How many frogs are there?

[12] frogs

② There are 4 grown-up rabbits. Each grown-up rabbit has 3 babies. How many rabbits are there in total?

[16] rabbits

③ How many birds are there?

[15] birds

43

④ Here are 20 monkeys. How many groups of 4 monkeys can you make? Put a circle around each group.

[5] groups

⑤ How many toes are there on four feet?

[20] toes

Counting in groups is the first step to recognizing that multiplication is quick addition. Children have two options: to count each thing individually or count how many things there are in each group and how many groups there are. Ex. 5 birds in 3 trees is 5 + 5 + 5 = 15.

Answers:

44–45 Charts
46–47 Money

44

Kim made a chart of the weather in one week.

Days of the Week	Weather
Monday	☀
Tuesday	☁
Wednesday	☀
Thursday	🌧
Friday	☀
Saturday	☀
Sunday	☁

☀ = Sunny

🌧 = Rainy

☁ = Cloudy

(1) What was the weather like on Wednesday? .... Sunny

(2) How many days had rain? .... 1 day

(3) Which days were cloudy? .... Tuesday and Sunday

45

(4) Use the chart opposite to fill in this bar graph.
Color in the number of days for each type of weather.

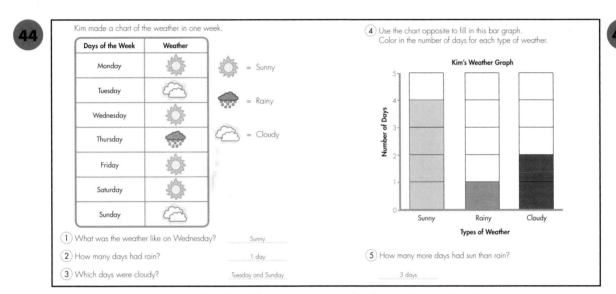

Kim's Weather Graph

Number of Days / Types of Weather

(5) How many more days had sun than rain?

.... 3 days

Weather is another popular subject for collecting data and creating charts and bar graphs. Children need to count carefully as they transfer data from the chart to the graph. Making comparisons between results is a useful way of interpreting data.

46

(1) Circle the two coins you would use to make 15 ¢.

1 ONE CENT   5 FIVE CENTS   10 TEN CENTS   25 TWENTY-FIVE CENTS

(2) Decrease each amount by 5 ¢.
Note: To decrease we subtract.

10 ¢	20 ¢	25 ¢	50 ¢
5 ¢	15 ¢	20 ¢	45 ¢

(3) Increase each amount by 3 ¢.
Note: To increase we add.

10 ¢	20 ¢	25 ¢	40 ¢
13 ¢	23 ¢	28 ¢	43 ¢

47

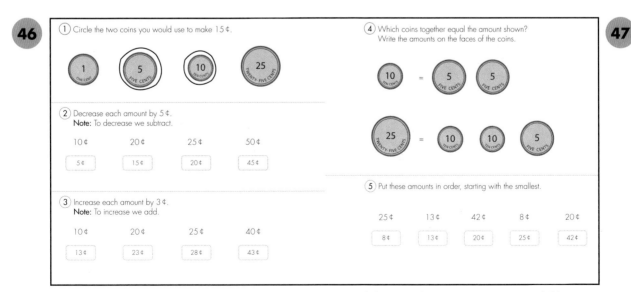

(4) Which coins together equal the amount shown?
Write the amounts on the faces of the coins.

10 = 5   5

25 = 10   10   5

(5) Put these amounts in order, starting with the smallest.

25 ¢	13 ¢	42 ¢	8 ¢	20 ¢
8 ¢	13 ¢	20 ¢	25 ¢	42 ¢

Provide children with a handful of coins to help them become familiar with their shapes and values. This visual aid will be useful as children increase and decrease the amounts. Encourage children to look at the tens and ones in numbers when comparing amounts.

Answers:

48–49 Fractions of Shapes
50–51 Solving Problems

48

① Color half the circle.

How many halves are there in a whole circle? `2`
Coloring may vary.

② Color a quarter of the rectangle.

How many quarters are there in a rectangle? `4`

③ Check (✔) the fraction colored on this circle.

$\frac{1}{2}$ ☐ $\frac{1}{4}$ ✔

49

④ Look at these shapes. Check (✔) the shapes that are half colored in.

✔

✔

⑤ Write a half as a fraction. `1` `2`

Write a quarter as a fraction. `1` `4`

At this age, children begin to partition circles and rectangles into two and four equal parts. They begin to use the terms half, fourths, and quarters. The bottom number of a fraction is the number of equal parts the whole is divided into, and the top number is the number of equal parts you have taken.

50

① James had 35 toy cars. John had 15 toy cars. How many toy cars did they have together?

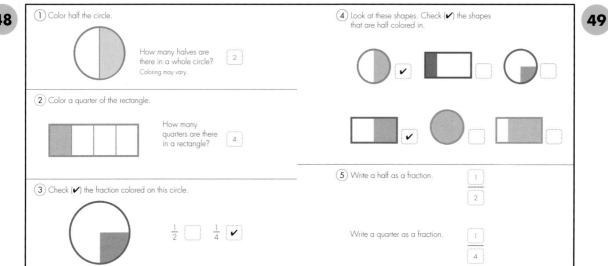

`50` cars

② Mom bought 8 oranges. Kate ate 2 of them. Jane ate 1. How many oranges were left?

`5` oranges

51

③ A lady had 3 cats. Each cat had 2 kittens. How many cats and kittens were there in total?

`9` cats and kittens

④ Omar had 40 books. He gave 26 to the school and the rest to charity. How many books did he give to charity?

`14` books

⑤ Dad cooked a pizza and cut it into 8 equal slices. He ate half of them. How many slices were left?

`4` slices

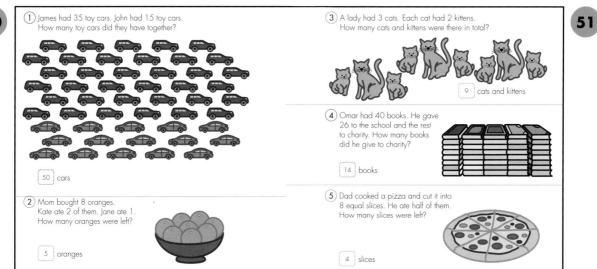

For the questions with larger numbers, encourage your children to use place value strategies to find the answers, ex. for 35 +15, add the tens 30 + 10 = 40 and then add the ones 5 + 5 = 10.

After that, add the two answers together: 40 + 10 = 50. Create your own questions so that your child can practice doing this.

Answers:

52–53 Shopping
54–55 Fractions of Amounts

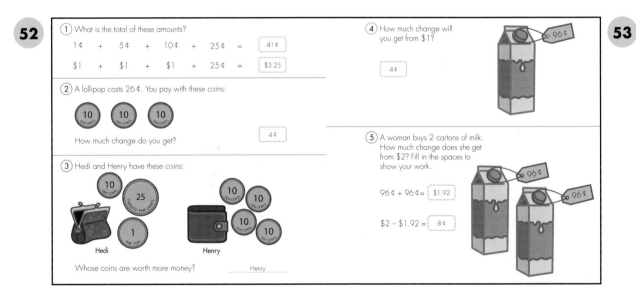

52

① What is the total of these amounts?

1¢ + 5¢ + 10¢ + 25¢ = 41¢

$1 + $1 + $1 + 25¢ = $3.25

② A lollipop costs 26¢. You pay with these coins:

How much change do you get? 4¢

③ Hedi and Henry have these coins:

Hedi   Henry

Whose coins are worth more money? Henry

53

④ How much change will you get from $1? 96¢

4¢

⑤ A woman buys 2 cartons of milk. How much change does she get from $2? Fill in the spaces to show your work. 96¢

96¢ + 96¢ = $1.92

$2 – $1.92 = 8¢

96¢

The final question requires two stages in working out the answer: finding the total cost of the two cartons; and then subtracting the answer from $2 to find the amount of change. Shopping provides a wonderful opportunity to talk about adding and subtracting, and comparing amounts.

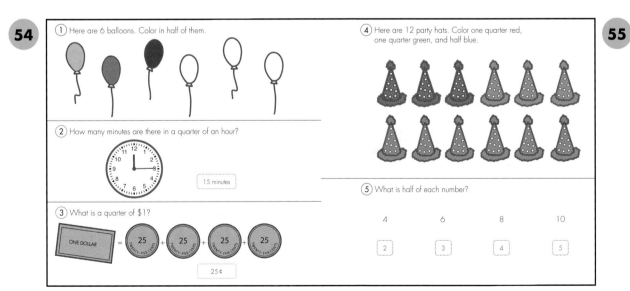

54

① Here are 6 balloons. Color in half of them.

② How many minutes are there in a quarter of an hour? 15 minutes

③ What is a quarter of $1?

ONE DOLLAR = 25 + 25 + 25 + 25

25¢

55

④ Here are 12 party hats. Color one quarter red, one quarter green, and half blue.

⑤ What is half of each number?

4   6   8   10

2   3   4   5

Children need to count or be aware of the amount of the whole before splitting the amount into half or quarters. For the last question, provide buttons or beads if it is necessary for your child to count and split equally.

Answers:

56–57 More Groups

58–59 More Time

56

1. How many fish are there? — `12` fish

2. There are 3 turtles. Each turtle lays 5 eggs. How many eggs are there? — `15` eggs

3. How many penguins are there? — `16` penguins

If children decide to count each animal individually that is fine at this grade. The concept of counting in groups as a faster way of adding will come later.

57

4. Here are 20 dolphins. How many groups of 5 dolphins can you make? Put a circle around each group. — `4` groups

5. Write the answers.

2 groups of 7 = `14`   3 groups of 10 = `30`

4 groups of 5 = `20`   5 groups of 3 = `15`

For question 5, they may wish to write down the question as an addition problem, ex. 2 groups of 7 would be the same as 7 + 7 = 14.

58

1. What time is it?

`10:30`   `11:30`   `4:30`

2. How many hours are there between these morning times?

`2 hours 30 minutes`

3. Jade started reading at 5 o'clock. She read for an hour. What time did she finish reading?

`6 o'clock`

These pages provide further practice in telling time and working out the difference between different times. For question 2, encourage children to count

59

4. Label this clock with numbers. Show 3 o'clock on the clock face.

5. School starts at 8:30. Dan left home at 8:00. How many minutes does he have to get to school on time?

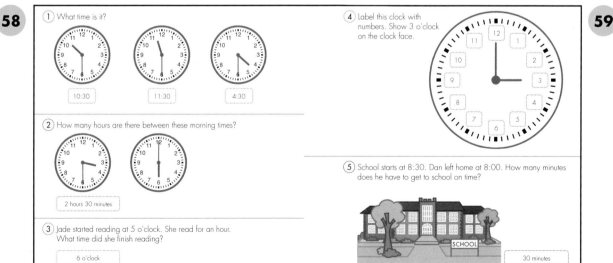

`30 minutes`

in hours and then add the last half an hour. Using a play clock can also help reinforce the differences between times.

Answers:

60–61 Racing Positions
62–63 Position

60

Six cars are racing.

(1) Which car is first? .... yellow car

(2) Which car is fourth? .... red car

61

(3) In what place is the green car?
.... second

(4) The cars line up in their finishing positions. Which car is fifth?
.... purple car

(5) Which car is lined up in front of the blue car?
.... purple car

Sports offers a wonderful opportunity to talk about numbers. Children can practice comparing numbers and adding/subtracting numbers while watching and/or playing sports. In this activity, ordinal math terms of first to sixth position are reinforced.

62

Look at this chart of animals.

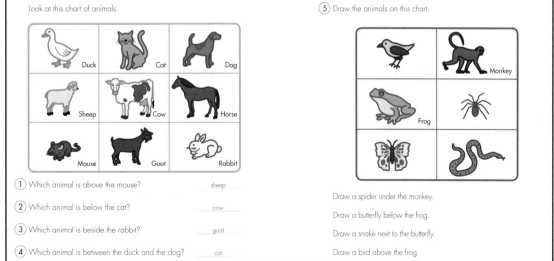

Duck	Cat	Dog
Sheep	Cow	Horse
Mouse	Goat	Rabbit

(1) Which animal is above the mouse? .... sheep

(2) Which animal is below the cat? .... cow

(3) Which animal is beside the rabbit? .... goat

(4) Which animal is between the duck and the dog? .... cat

63

(5) Draw the animals on this chart.

Bird	Monkey
Frog	Spider
Butterfly	Snake

Draw a spider under the monkey.

Draw a butterfly below the frog.

Draw a snake next to the butterfly.

Draw a bird above the frog.

These pages reinforce early math vocabulary to describe how animals are positioned in relation to one another. In later years, this skill will be transferred to looking at shapes positioned on a grid.

Answers:

20–21 Beat the Clock 1
40–41 Beat the Clock 2
64–65 Beat the Clock 3

These pages test your child's mental math skills. Although these questions are answered against the clock, children should not feel pressured to rush their answers. It is more important to be accurate as they could try again and beat the clock another time. You may want to record the time taken on each try.

20 – 21

1	11	2	5	3	60	31	3	32	9	33	66
4	17	5	46	6	80	34	29	35	2	36	20
7	13	8	87	9	50	37	38	38	6	39	55
10	22	11	57	12	64	40	44	41	78	42	81
13	7	14	92	15	12	43	30	44	19	45	27
16	15	17	10	18	4	46	52	47	98	48	8
19	18	20	49	21	61	49	1	50	91	51	40
22	41	23	39	24	93	52	35	53	16	54	75
25	77	26	83	27	24	55	84	56	74	57	33
28	100	29	21	30	32	58	53	59	14	60	59

40 – 41

1	5	2	11	3	9	31	15	32	19	33	12
4	8	5	12	6	17	34	18	35	17	36	16
7	8	8	10	9	13	37	20	38	18	39	12
10	13	11	10	12	12	40	20	41	20	42	9
13	11	14	16	15	20	43	20	44	22	45	12
16	14	17	7	18	14	46	12	47	23	48	15
19	6	20	13	21	15	49	20	50	20	51	20
22	8	23	13	24	18	52	18	53	20	54	19
25	11	26	15	27	13	55	17	56	18	57	20
28	15	29	18	30	22	58	14	59	19	60	28

64 – 65

1	5	2	1	3	2	31	7	32	11	33	4
4	4	5	0	6	10	34	11	35	9	36	9
7	3	8	2	9	5	37	4	38	13	39	3
10	8	11	4	12	12	40	7	41	8	42	4
13	3	14	6	15	2	43	6	44	9	45	3
16	1	17	0	18	10	46	7	47	12	48	8
19	2	20	7	21	12	49	10	50	11	51	6
22	7	23	2	24	11	52	6	53	9	54	2
25	1	26	4	27	3	55	1	56	7	57	10
28	3	29	1	30	6	58	5	59	12	60	5